Fly

Written by
David Lindo

Illustrated by
Sara Boccaccini Meadows

MAGIC CAT 🐾 PUBLISHING

Birds have fascinated us humans since the dawn of time. Over the generations we have celebrated them in many different ways: We have written songs about them, drawn and painted them, created mythology around them, domesticated them, and even named buildings, streets, and towns after them.

But despite this fascination, we have also been quite destructive toward birds. We have hunted them, polluted our rivers and seas, and destroyed huge swaths of their habitat.

I hope that this book will help readers connect with the wonderful world of birds and realize what a diverse a group of animals they are. Birds don't have to possess gaudy plumages to be interesting: The plain-colored ones make up for their dowdiness with their incredible stories and intriguing behavioral traits. It is these stories that I want to share.

We know quite a lot about the lives of birds now, but there are still big gaps in our knowledge. I am hoping that after reading this book you will want to go out and study the the birds that you see to find out more about their lives. It's a common misconception that you have to venture into the middle of the countryside to do this. It can start from your backyard, your local park, your home city.

In 1943, David Lack decided to study the European robins in his neighborhood in Oxford, England. He wasn't a scientist, but his discoveries about the robin now shape what we know and take for granted today. We can all make such discoveries about even the most common of birds that surround us. We can all enjoy birds.

Get outside and look up!

—D.L.

CONTENTS

 2 — The HERO of **FABULOUS FEATHERS**
the GREAT ARGUS

 6 — The HERO of **FANTASTIC FEET**
the HARPY EAGLE

 10 — The HERO of **EYE-CATCHING COLOR**
the PARADISE TANAGER

 14 — The HERO of **WONDERFUL WINGS**
the WANDERING ALBATROSS

 18 — The HERO of **BRILLIANT BEAKS**
the SHOEBILL

 22 — The HERO of **NIFTY NESTS**
the MALLEEFOWL

 26 — The HERO of **FRIENDLY FLOCKS**
the LESSER FLAMINGO

 30 — The HERO of **AMAZING MIGRATIONS**
the BAR-TAILED GODWIT

 34 — The HERO of **WATER WORLDS**
the ADÉLIE PENGUIN

 38 — The HERO of **DRY DESERTS**
the CROWNED SANDGROUSE

 42 — The HERO of **WILD WOODLANDS**
the BLACKBURNIAN WARBLER

 46 — The HERO of **THE OPEN OCEAN**
the SOOTY SHEARWATER

 50 — The HERO of **GRASSLANDS**
the CHESTNUT-COLLARED LONGSPUR

 54 — The HERO of **THE URBAN JUNGLE**
the PEREGRINE FALCON

 58 — The HERO of **CONSERVATION**
the KAKAPO

62 — **GLOSSARY**

GREAT ARGUS
ARGUSIANUS ARGUS

Feathers come in all different shapes and sizes, and every shade of color that you can imagine. The spectacular-looking great argus is a member of the pheasant family. The male will stalk around a female splaying his amazing plumes at her to try to win her affection.

PREENING
A bird will preen several times a day to keep its feathers in tip-top condition. The bird can remove dust, dirt, and parasites from its plumage by spreading a special oil with its beak from a preen gland at the base of its tail. By doing this essential work the bird can stay healthy, attractive, and better waterproofed.

The great argus is one of the world's **largest pheasants.** The male is much bigger than the female.

male

A male's tail can be nearly 5 feet long. His very long secondary wing feathers are adorned with large **eyespots**.

HOW TO SPOT
This impressive pheasant is found in the jungles of Borneo and Sumatra in Southeast Asia. The male displays in forest clearings, announcing himself with loud cries. He then dances before the female, spreading his enormous feathers so that his hundreds of eyespots are staring right at her!

ALL ABOUT FEATHERS

Feathers grow from a bird's skin and are lightweight structures that are connected by small hooked branches called barbules.

barbules

A bird has thousands of feathers covering its body. This is known as its plumage.

Some birds, like vultures, have featherless heads to keep them clean when feeding on a carcass.

KING-OF-SAXONY BIRD-OF-PARADISE
Birds-of-paradise are famous for their feathers. This species has unusual **brow plumes**.

Pteridophora alberti

Aythya fuligula

TUFTED DUCK
This **diving duck** sports its tuft in towns and cities in Europe and Alaska.

Calidris pugnax

RUFF
Named for their neck feathers, breeding male ruffs show off their **feathery ruffs** a few weeks a year in communal display sites called leks.

ADAPTATION

LENGTHENED FEATHERS
The male **pennant-winged nightjar** is very distinctive thanks to its pennant feathers, which grow to be twice as long as its body in the breeding season. It shows them off as it flies overhead to impress females during courtship displays, then loses them after mating.

Caprimulgus vexillarius

MARVELOUS SPATULETAIL

This adorable hummingbird has a brilliant **tail** with two long, bare shafts.

Loddigesia mirabilis

EURASIAN HOOPOE

This strange bird has one of the most unusual **crests** in the whole bird world.

Upupa epops

FEATHERS AROUND THE WORLD

The great argus was given its name due to the numerous eyelike patterns on its elongated wing feathers. Argus was a **hundred-eyed giant** in Greek mythology.

Eagle feathers are traditionally presented to the bravest, strongest, and holiest members of **Indigenous American communities**.

In ancient Egypt, the goddess **Ma'at** would weigh a dead person's heart against an ostrich feather on the scales of justice. If the heart was heavy with sin, then the person would not be admitted into paradise.

FABULOUS FEATHERS

HARPY EAGLE
HARPIA HARPYJA

A bird's claws are made from keratin, like our toenails. Some birds have four toes, perfect for gripping branches, while others, like the American three-toed woodpecker, have just three... And the ostrich is the only bird with just two toes! Most impressive of all are the huge feet belonging to the harpy eagle.

MONSTER FEET

This shy eagle is one of the biggest raptors in the world. The female harpy's feet are the size of a human hand, with huge, 5-inch-long talons that are often longer than those of a grizzly bear!

HOW TO SPOT

The harpy eagle lives in the rainforests of Central and South America.

It tends to fly within the forest canopy or just above it, making it very hard to detect, but you might catch a lucky glimpse of this magnificent eagle near its nesting site.

Harpies also have very sharp **eyesight**—eight times better than ours—which they use to locate their prey before capturing it with their formidable feet.

The **female** is much larger than the male and can weigh up to 20 pounds.

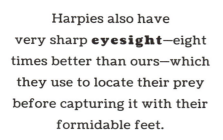
female

These birds do not spend much time flying in search of prey. Instead, they sit and **wait** for an unfortunate monkey to pass by before silently swooping on it.

A harpy's feet and **talons** are so strong that it can easily lift prey as heavy as itself.

ALL ABOUT FEET

Birds' feet are adapted to their environments: Waterbirds often have webbed feet for swimming; perching birds have small, strong feet for gripping branches; and flightless birds have sturdy feet for walking.

MALLARD
The most common duck in the world probably has the most famous **webbed feet**, which are great for moving in water but less so on solid ground.

Anas platyrhynchos

AMERICAN ROBIN
The robin is what's known as a **perching bird**, with toes pointing forward and backward for gripping.

Turdus migratorius

Hydrophasianus chirurgus

Apus apus

COMMON SWIFT
This bird's scientific name means "footless footless." In actual fact, a swift has **clinging feet**, evolved to grip the sides of cliffs.

PHEASANT-TAILED JACANA
This aquatic bird has really **long toes** that spread its weight and stop it from sinking!

COMMON OSTRICH
The ostrich can reach speeds of 43 miles per hour when running and is the fastest bird on **two legs**.

Struthio camelus

SECRETARYBIRD
The secretarybird spends most of its time on the ground and kills snakes by stomping on them. It has **hunting feet** with razor-sharp claws, designed to cling tightly to prey.

Sagittarius serpentarius

FEET AROUND THE WORLD

The harpy eagle is named after **Harpies** in Greek mythology, who were fearsome creatures with female human heads and birds' bodies.

A Roman story described a **crane** keeping vigil while holding a rock in its raised foot; if the crane were to fall asleep, it would drop its rock and wake up.

This symbol of vigilance is seen in many heraldic **crests**, including that of the Scottish clan Cranstoun.

A **three-legged crow** is present in many East Asian myths and is associated with the sun.

Swan and geese feet sometimes feature in European myths. Both Freyja, the Norse goddess, and Berchta, the fierce German goddess, have been depicted with only one human foot and one foot of a goose, while the lamia in Basque mythology had the **webbed feet** of a duck.

ADAPTATION

COLD FEET

Have you ever wondered if a bird gets cold feet in freezing weather? Well, its feet are cold, but the bird doesn't feel it because it has very little fluid, muscles, or nerves in its legs and feet.

Some birds, like the **snowy owl**, have feathered feet. Like warm, fluffy slippers, the extra insulation protects against the cold.

Warm blood flows from the owl's body into the legs via an artery and then cools. But when the blood returns to its body through a vein, it warms up again, keeping the bird nice and toasty.

Bubo scandiacus

FANTASTIC FEET   9   FANTASTIC FEET

the HERO of EYE-CATCHING COLOR

the PARADISE TANAGER

Many kinds of animal—from mammals to reptiles and amphibians—have evolved to blend in subtly with their surroundings, but birds are among the most colorful animals on the planet! Brightest of all is the paradise tanager.

PARADISE TANAGER
Tangara chilensis

Birds are colorful for many reasons. Bright feathers can help birds of the same species recognize each other. Their feathers can tell predators that they are bad-tasting or poisonous. And sometimes birds use their bright plumes to attract possible mates.

COLORFUL CAMOUFLAGE

Surprisingly, bright colors can sometimes camouflage a bird. Despite its brightness, a paradise tanager can be very difficult to spot when foraging for insects and fruit because of the bright, lush, tropical plant life found in its habitat.

male

Often, males will sport **brighter** colors than females of the same species, to help them attract a mate.

In its native habitat, this bird is also called the **seven-colored tanager**, thanks to its green, turquoise, blue, yellow, red, gray, and black feathers.

Unusually, both the male and female paradise tanager appear to have **similar plumage**...

...but in **ultraviolet light**, male and female birds look quite different and can easily tell each other apart.

HOW TO SPOT
The paradise tanager is the jewel of the Amazon Basin.

The best way to see this species is to visit the specially established feeding stations, where many birds that are normally quite shy—including the paradise tanager—come to feast on the fruit left out for them.

EYE-CATCHING COLOR

ALL ABOUT COLOR

What makes a bird's plumage colorful? Well, its feathers contain two types of pigments. Firstly, melanins, which produce a range of black, gray, brown, and orange colors, and secondly, carotenoids, which generate brighter color tones.

Tragopan melanocephalus

WESTERN TRAGOPAN
Some birds have colorful patches of **skin,** like this tragopan whose featherless face features vibrant colors.

Tachuris rubrigastra

MANY-COLORED RUSH TYRANT
This tiny South American bird has brightly colored feathers that are green, blue, red, yellow, white, and black . . . hence its **name**!

Merops apiaster

EUROPEAN BEE-EATER
Bee-eaters are a family of birds that feed almost exclusively on **bees,** hornets, and wasps.

Passerina ciris

PAINTED BUNTING
Male painted buntings only acquire their bright feathers in their **second year of life**.

Agamia agami

AGAMI HERON
With its beautiful **slate-blue** feathers, this is perhaps the most beautiful heron in the world.

Aix galericulata

MANDARIN DUCK
Very few waterbirds are as colorful as this tree-nesting **forest dweller** in Asia.

COLORFUL BIRDS AROUND THE WORLD

The scarlet-and-gold **phoenix** is an immortal bird associated with Greek and Egyptian mythology. It gains new life when it rises from the dead in a shower of red flames.

In Germany, the mythical **Hercinia** (or arcinee) was said to live in the Hercynian Forest. Its plumage glowed like fire or sparks in the night and helped light the way for travelers.

In a Flemish folk story, the **rainbow finch** won her colors after waiting patiently when the Great Bird invited all the birds to pick their colors from the rainbow. The finch was left with none, so the Great Bird called back all the others and took a bit of color from each, making the finch the prettiest of all.

ADAPTATION

ULTRAVIOLET VISION

Some birds, like the **malachite kingfisher**, have eyes that are able to detect near-ultraviolet light from the sun, allowing them to see other birds' plumages in an even more dazzling way. The structure of their eyes has an adaptation that humans do not have that allows them to detect the light.

Corythornis cristatus

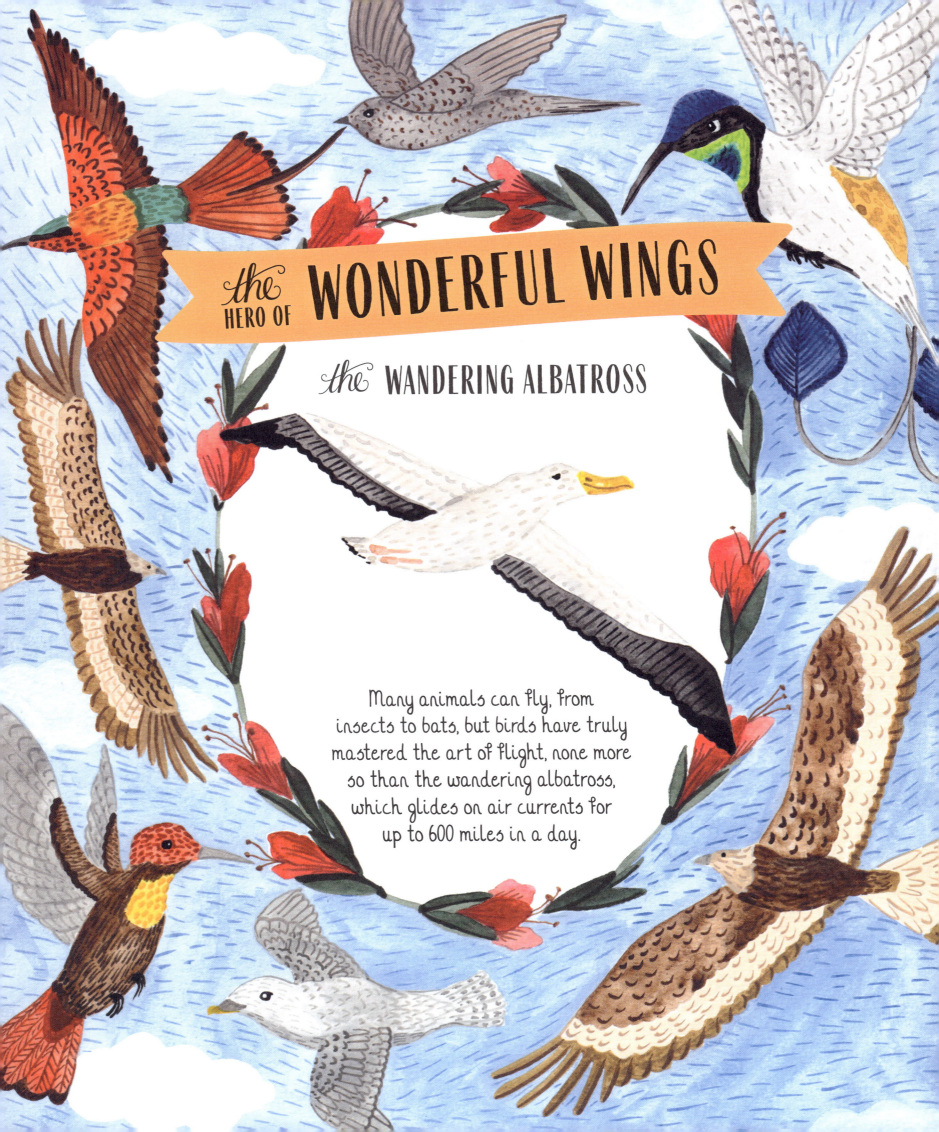

WANDERING ALBATROSS
Diomedea exulans

Every bird has a pair of wings—even those that can't fly! But how do birds actually fly? Birds like albatrosses have lightweight, aerodynamic bodies, hollow bones, and sleek feathers. They use their wings to create lift and their tails as rudders, making them masters of the skies.

POWERED FLIGHT
Wandering albatrosses power their flight by using their incredibly strong chest muscles, known as pectoral muscles. For humans to fly, we would need a wingspan of up to 23 feet and huge pectoral muscles projecting more than 3 feet out from our rib cages!

At up to 12 feet, this species boasts the **longest wingspan** of any living bird in the world.

This species has been known to circumnavigate the Antarctic Ocean **three times** a year, covering more than 74,000 miles.

This bird is so **efficient** at flying that it can remain in the air without flapping for several hours at a time, using less energy there than it does sitting on a nest.

These birds only come to land once every **two years** to breed on islands in the Antarctic Ocean.

HOW TO SPOT
The best way to see these giant birds is to visit their breeding grounds.
They lay just one egg in sheltered areas around sub-Antarctic islands. Otherwise, you have to try to spot one from a ship as it flies in search of food. You could be in luck, though, as they like following vessels in the hope of receiving scraps from the sailors.

ALL ABOUT WINGS

Birds have evolved a variety of different wing shapes to help them fly. Generally speaking, birds with long and narrow wings like the albatross are experts at gliding.

Columba palumbus

COMMON WOOD PIGEON

Some birds use their wings to communicate with their flock members. When startled, pigeons noisily explode from trees, loudly **clapping** their wings to alert others.

Machaeropterus deliciosus

CLUB-WINGED MANAKIN

This is the only bird known to **sing** with its wings! When displaying, males first flatten their wings, then snap them upright, which produces a buzz as hollowed feathers on their wings rub together.

Opisthocomus hoazin

HOATZIN

As a young chick, this odd-looking bird has a claw on the bend of each wing, which helps it clamber up waterside vegetation.

BLACK-BREASTED KITE

This kite has broad-fingered wings, typical of birds of prey, that help it **ride** hot air thermals and to swiftly power after its prey.

Hamirostra melanosternon

Egretta ardesiaca

Loddigesia mirabilis

MARVELOUS SPATULETAIL

This minute hummingbird can flap its wings up to 70 times a second, and, like the rest of its family, it can even fly **backward**.

BLACK HERON

This bird opens its wings like an **umbrella** when hunting small fish, luring them in by creating a patch of shade beneath it.

ADAPTATION

Rupicola rupicola

DISPLAY FEATHERS

Some birds, including the **Guianan cock-of-the-rock**, use their wings as part of their courtship displays. To attract a female, the male performs an elaborate ritual, fanning his wings to show off his stunning feathers.

WINGS AROUND THE WORLD

The wandering albatross's scientific name, *Diomedea exulans*, refers to **Diomedes**, a hero in Greek mythology whose companions were turned into shearwaters (relatives of albatrosses).

According to a **Persian fable**, King Kai Kawus tried to invade heaven on a throne with four hungry eagles chained to its legs. Each leg had a pole with meat on top. The eagles used their powerful wings to fly toward the meat, carrying the throne upward.

In an **Indian folktale**, elephants originally had four big wings and would cause destruction by landing on people's houses and crushing them.

The gods decided to stop the mayhem and cut the wings off, giving two to the **peacocks** and two to the banana plant, which is why its leaves are so large!

SHOEBILL
Balaeniceps rex

Birds do not have mouths or teeth. Instead, they have beaks that are made of bone with a covering of keratin, which is what your fingernails are made of. Like your nails, a bird's beak never stops growing. It is kept at the right shape and size through continual use.

BEAK OF ALL BEAKS!
The shoebill's enormous beak looks like a Dutch clog. It measures 9 inches long and 4 inches wide at its base.

Its beak has a serious **sharp hook** at the tip, and its edges are just as sharp: perfect for catching and hanging on to prey!

These **waterbirds** use that humongous beak to scoop up and eat large fish.

If a shoebill's eggs get too hot, the parent will **collect water** in its beak and pour it over the eggs to keep them cool.

HOW TO SPOT
Shoebills live alongside rivers in the marshes and swamps of East and Central Africa.

They often stand on floating vegetation or along the water's edge like statues, not moving a muscle until they spot some prey like a large fish. Because their habitat is so hard to penetrate, the shoebill is the visiting birdwatcher's most sought-after bird in the whole of Africa.

ALL ABOUT BEAKS

Birds' beaks have mainly evolved to help them specialize in eating certain foods—in fact, it was by examining the differently shaped beaks of finches that Charles Darwin came up with his theory of evolution.

Aulacorhynchus prasinus

EMERALD TOUCANET
Fruit eaters like this Central American toucan sport beaks that are a variety of shapes and sizes, and excellent for plucking fruit.

Haliaeetus pelagicus

AMERICAN OYSTERCATCHER
Like other **probers**, this shorebird has a long beak used to delve into the mud to search for invertebrate prey, including shellfish, crabs, starfish, and sea urchins.

Haematopus palliatus

STELLER'S SEA EAGLE
Predators, like this huge eagle from northeastern Asia, have strong, sharp, hooked beaks that are ideal for ripping up flesh.

EVENING GROSBEAK
This North American finch is a **seedeater**, with a thick and strong conical beak for cracking open nuts and seeds.

Coccothraustes vespertinus

Ardea herodias

Ensifera ensifera

SWORD-BILLED HUMMINGBIRD
This South American **nectar feeder** has the longest bill of any bird in relation to its size, which it plunges into flowers with long corollas (petals).

GREAT BLUE HERON
This large North American **fish catcher** slowly stalks along riverbanks before lunging at fish in a lightning-fast strike.

BEAKS AROUND THE WORLD

The **woodpecker** was associated with Thor, god of thunder and lightning in Norse mythology. While Thor had a magic hammer, a woodpecker hammers on trees.

In Iroquois mythology, **ducks** dived underwater and used their flattened beaks to bring up mud to create an island for a female deity.

The yellowish horns on the bill of the **rhinoceros hornbill** represent virility and male dominance to the Dayak community on the island of Borneo.

One Brazilian legend says that **toucans** saw themselves as the kings of all birds because of their enormous bills.

ADAPTATION

SPATULATE BILL

Filterers like this **roseate spoonbill** have specially adapted beaks that help them sieve their food from the water or mud. They wade through the water, sweeping their partially open bill and snapping it shut if they detect a tasty morsel.

Platalea ajaja

MALLEEFOWL
Leipoa ocellata

The unremarkable-looking malleefowl certainly makes a remarkable-looking nest! The chicken-size male constructs a large mound, 13 feet across and 3 feet tall. The female then lays her eggs within it and never returns to care for her chicks.

ABSENT PARENTS

The malleefowl nest is constructed by the male. He scrapes a hollow with his feet, fills it with twigs, leaves, and bark, and waits for rain. After it has rained, he mixes the mushy material to help it decay, then covers it with sand. He then digs a chamber where the female lays her eggs.

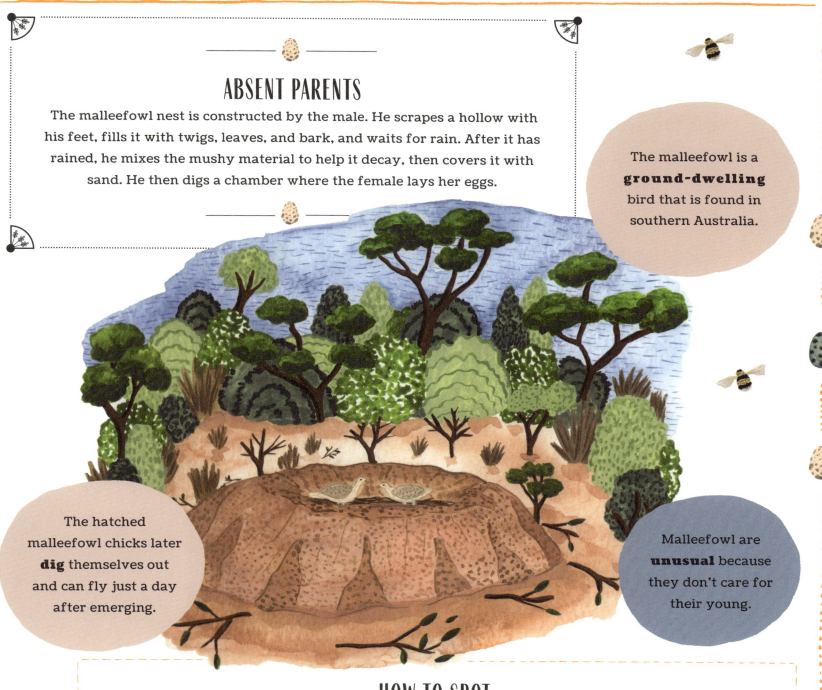

The malleefowl is a **ground-dwelling** bird that is found in southern Australia.

The hatched malleefowl chicks later **dig** themselves out and can fly just a day after emerging.

Malleefowl are **unusual** because they don't care for their young.

HOW TO SPOT

The strange malleefowl lives in the semiarid mallee scrub found in only a few areas of southern Australia... but you may find them tricky to spot!

Mallee is the name given to the general growth of small trees and woody shrubs typical of the bird's habitat. You will have difficulty finding them because, despite being very active, they freeze if they are disturbed, relying on their intricately patterned plumage for camouflage, or they will rapidly and silently slip into the undergrowth.

NIFTY NESTS — 23 — NIFTY NESTS

ALL ABOUT NESTS

Birds usually build their nests using vegetation, sometimes weaving them together elaborately and lining them with soft materials like feathers. Some species also decorate their nests with stones and even our plastic waste, while others build their nests using mud.

Erithacus rubecula

EUROPEAN ROBIN

European robins are famous for nesting in **strange places** like discarded teapots.

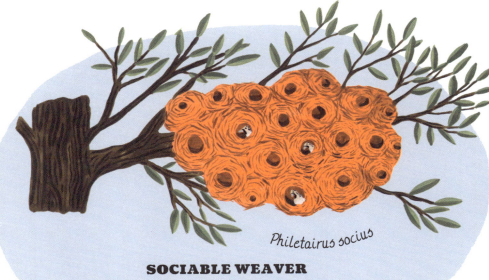

Philetairus socius

SOCIABLE WEAVER

Weavers in Africa nest **communally**. Their separate nests join together like a giant housing estate!

ADAPTATION

Gygis alba

BARE NESTS

The **white tern** doesn't bother with a nest. Instead, it carefully balances its egg on the fork of a bare branch. Scientists aren't completely sure why it does this, but think it could be to avoid parasites in its nest, which is a common problem for other seabirds living in colonies.

NESTS AROUND THE WORLD

In many northern European legends, prosperity will come to any home that finds a bird's nest among the branches of the family **Christmas tree**.

Podilymbus podiceps

PIED-BILLED GREBE
Some aquatic birds like grebes build **floating** nests that sometimes incorporate trash that humans have thrown into the waterways.

Aptenodytes forsteri

EMPEROR PENGUIN
The emperor penguin uses its own **body** to protect its egg from the icy cold. It balances its egg on the top of its feet and covers it with its warm downy feathers.

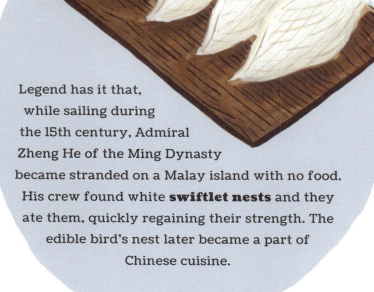

Legend has it that, while sailing during the 15th century, Admiral Zheng He of the Ming Dynasty became stranded on a Malay island with no food. His crew found white **swiftlet nests** and they ate them, quickly regaining their strength. The edible bird's nest later became a part of Chinese cuisine.

Some German and Dutch homeowners have been known to place high platforms on their roofs to encourage **storks** to build nests because they believe the birds bring good luck.

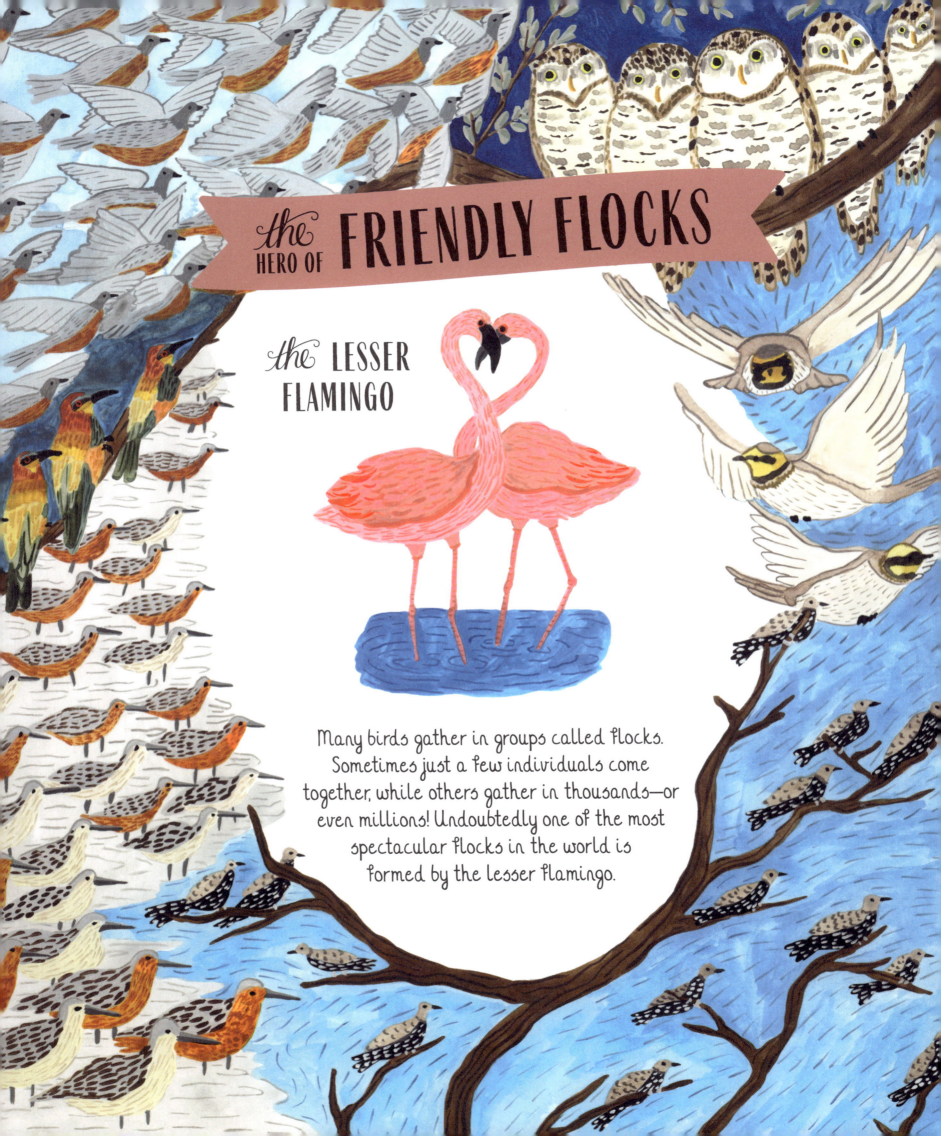

the HERO OF FRIENDLY FLOCKS

the LESSER FLAMINGO

Many birds gather in groups called flocks. Sometimes just a few individuals come together, while others gather in thousands—or even millions! Undoubtedly one of the most spectacular flocks in the world is formed by the lesser flamingo.

LESSER FLAMINGO
Phoeniconaias minor

Birds usually flock for protection against predators. Being together in such large numbers makes it harder for a predator to pick out one bird, especially with so many eyes watching out for danger. The glamorous flamingo gathers in huge flocks to breed on shallow salty lakes and coastal lagoons.

SAFETY IN NUMBERS
The lesser flamingo, like many other species of bird, nests together in flocks. A group of these distinctive birds is known as a flamboyance of flamingos.

These gorgeous-looking birds have a poor sense of smell and taste but have good **eyesight**.

Flocks **communicate** using their voices and by flashing their wing feathers at each other.

A few days after hatching, chicks join a **crèche**, often numbering thousands. Other flamingos watch them while their parents find food.

HOW TO SPOT
Around three-quarters of the world's population of lesser flamingos flock to the very alkaline waters of Lake Natron in Tanzania, Africa.

The hypersaline water is so toxic here that it would strip the skin from your body if you were to swim in it! Yet the flamingos flourish! Tough skin on their legs and feet protects them from being burned, and they can drink the hot, salty water—which can rise to 140 degrees Fahrenheit—and drain the salt through special glands in their noses. Crucially, flamingos are able to digest the poisonous algae living in the water, and this gives the birds their pink color!

ALL ABOUT FLOCKS

Birds flock for many reasons. Some, like flamingos, form huge breeding flocks; others gather to make the most of an abundant food source, while some migrate in vast numbers.

BRAMBLING
Bramblings form tremendous **winter-feeding** flocks numbering millions in northern Europe.

Fringilla montifringilla

Sturnus vulgaris

STARLING
Starlings gather in flocks called **murmurations**, which seem to play, creating incredible shapes in the air before plunging down into their roosts.

CHIMNEY SWIFT
These sociable birds appear to perform a magic trick at the end of the day as they disappear by the thousands in a tornado-like flurry, returning to their **roosts**, which are often in tall, vertical spaces such as chimneys.

Chaetura pelagica

COLLECTIVE NOUNS
Flocking birds have names—called collective nouns—given to their specific groups such as a "parliament of owls" and an "exaltation of larks."

Ectopistes migratorius

PASSENGER PIGEON
The largest flocks of birds ever recorded were made up of the now sadly **extinct** North American passenger pigeon. These flocks were so vast that they would darken the sky, reaching over a mile wide, 300 miles long, and taking many hours to pass.

ADAPTATION

MIXED-SPECIES FLOCKS

Birds can form mixed-species flocks, especially when they are foraging for food or migrating. You can observe these groups in woodlands and forests, with species cooperating in the search for food and watching out for predators. **Wading birds** and **seabirds** can share the same behavior, with different species flocking together.

FLOCKS AROUND THE WORLD

Stymphalian birds were a group of monstrous creatures in Greek mythology that swarmed over the countryside destroying crops, fruit trees, and townspeople.

British coal-mining communities shared a folktale about the **Seven Whistlers**, a group of mysterious wading birds that flew together at night and whose unearthly calls forewarned of disaster.

It is said that the collective noun **"murder of crows"** may have come from a folktale: Groups of crows would sit in judgment on a member of the flock. If found guilty, the bird would be murdered by the rest of the flock.

FRIENDLY FLOCKS

the HERO OF AMAZING MIGRATIONS

the BAR-TAILED GODWIT

Birds embark on some of the most amazing migrations on the planet, and one of the most incredible journeys is undertaken by the bar-tailed godwit.

BAR-TAILED GODWIT
Limosa lapponica

Different bird species migrate in different ways. They can undertake their journey alone, in small groups, or in vast flocks. They might glide, flap, swim, or even walk, travel by night or day, and can spend hours, days, months, or even years on the move.

RECORD-BREAKERS

The elegant bar-tailed godwit performs the longest nonstop migration of any bird, traveling an average of more than 6,800 miles.

Some bar-tailed godwits **fly nonstop** from Alaska to Australia and New Zealand. The journey takes between nine and eleven days.

The birds prepare for migration by eating a lot and storing the fat to give them **energy**. Their stomachs shrink and their flight muscles increase in size before they set off.

Unlike birds such as the albatross, which glide, the godwit **actively moves** its wings for the whole of its mammoth journey. Imagine flapping your arms nonstop for more than a week!

HOW TO SPOT

More than 90,000 bar-tailed godwits—many just a few months old—depart from their western and northern Alaskan breeding grounds.

Some birds stop over in New Caledonia or Australia, while others keep going all the way to New Zealand. The birds take a different route on the return journey, landing in South Korea for a rest before completing their journey back to Alaska.

ALL ABOUT MIGRATIONS

Around 40 percent of the world's birds migrate to some extent. Birds migrate for a variety of reasons, but the main one is food supply.

Smaller birds tend to travel by night to avoid predation, while larger birds like hawks and storks travel by day, riding the hot air thermals.

COMMON SWIFT
Swifts spend just a few short months in Europe, to breed and raise their **chicks**, before returning to southern Africa. When these birds leave their nests, they can spend up to four years on the wing until they stop to breed.

Apus apus

WESTERN YELLOW WAGTAIL
These insect-eating birds breed in northern areas, then move south when their food supply begins to disappear in the autumn. They return in the spring when the weather is warmer and the **insects** have become more abundant.

Motacilla flava

ARCTIC TERN
This species migrates **farther** than any other bird. It breeds in the Arctic and migrates to Antarctica, flying more than 20,000 miles in a year and seeing more daylight than any other creature on Earth.

Sterna paradisaea

Aptenodytes forsteri

EMPEROR PENGUIN
These birds spend part of their migration walking or **sliding** on their bellies over the ice before reaching the sea.

WILLOW PTARMIGAN
Not all birds migrate vast distances. Some, like these mountain-loving birds, simply travel to **lower elevations** to escape the harsh conditions farther up.

Lagopus lagopus

ADAPTATION

Columba livia domestica

NAVIGATION

Migrating birds instinctively know in what direction to travel. They also use the sun, stars, and Earth's magnetic field to guide them. **Homing pigeons** have an especially remarkable ability to navigate their way home. Scientists are still trying to figure out how they do it! It may involve multiple sensory mechanisms, including an ability to sense the intensity of Earth's magnetic field thanks to a small spot in the birds' beaks that contains magnetite.

MIGRATIONS AROUND THE WORLD

The godwit is a sacred bird in Māori tradition. The birds, known as **kuaka**, were thought to pass through the Māori ancestral home, Hawaiki, on their migratory journey.

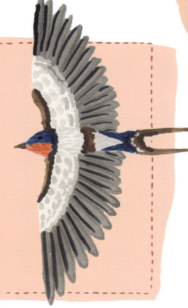

Before ornithologists knew that birds migrated, it was believed that barn swallows spent the winter **buried** at the bottom of ponds.

The swallow's annual return is often celebrated cautiously, with the **ancient Greek proverb**: "One swallow does not a summer make."

In southern Africa, Zulu, Sesotho, and Tswana peoples traditionally believed that migrating birds would fatten the land and bring the **rains** with their arrival.

The 17th-century English scientist Charles Morton mistakenly thought that birds flew to the **moon** to spend the winter. He estimated that it would take 60 days for them to get there.

AMAZING MIGRATIONS — 33 — AMAZING MIGRATIONS

the HERO OF WATER WORLDS
the ADÉLIE PENGUIN

Birds may be known as masters of the skies, but they rule the waves, too! Though penguins can't fly, underwater, they really spread their wings... or flippers, to be exact!

ADÉLIE PENGUIN
PYGOSCELIS ADELIAE

Like other aquatic birds, penguins are well adapted to swimming. They have a streamlined body, webbed feet, and dense waterproof plumage that keeps them warm and helps them glide through their watery world. They are expert divers and can go to depths of 575 feet in search of fish!

FLYING UNDERWATER
When diving underwater, penguins **flap their wings** to propel themselves after their prey.

A penguin's distinctive black-and-white plumage helps **camouflage** it against the light of the sun from below and the dark sea from above.

Adélie penguins live in large colonies of up to 1.5 million birds. The oldest colony is at least **6,335 years old**!

These penguins are excellent walkers, traveling 30 miles or more across the ice. They can also **toboggan** over snowy, open terrain on their bellies.

HOW TO SPOT
Adélie penguins are among the most difficult to find despite being the most common penguin species. This is because most of the population breed on difficult-to-access ice shelves and peninsulas in Antarctica. Visiting the colonies is strictly controlled and you are not allowed to touch the penguins, to prevent diseases being transmitted to the birds.

ALL ABOUT WATERBIRDS

Waterbirds are found in wetland habitats such as marshes, rivers, ponds, lakes, and shorelines, where they can feed, rest, and nest. You can even find waterbirds in the middle of urban areas with parks and canals.

Anser indicus

BAR-HEADED GOOSE

Despite being a web-footed waterbird, the bar-headed goose is a highflier in the bird world, having been recorded migrating at an altitude of over 29,000 feet!

AMERICAN COOT

This waterbird has peculiar lobed **webbed toes** that help propel it through the water.

Fulica americana

Rhodonessa caryophyllacea

PINK-HEADED DUCK

This bird might still live on the plains by the River Ganges in India and Bangladesh, or in the swamps of Myanmar, but it is so rare and **secretive** that it has not been seen since 1949.

WATERBIRDS AROUND THE WORLD

The **caladrius** is a waterbird from Roman mythology and medieval folklore that would appear when someone was sick to absorb the disease from that person.

The shape-shifting **boobrie** from Scotland was a malevolent mythological creature that attacked otters and could transform into a giant insect to suck the blood of horses.

WATER WORLDS — 36 — WATER WORLDS

Cygnus melancoryphus

BLACK-NECKED SWAN

A swan parent keeps its young **cygnets** safe on its back by carrying them as it swims through the water, helping the chicks conserve energy.

Heliornis fulica

SUNGREBE

This species lives almost exclusively on water and has **adapted** so well to its environment that it finds it difficult to walk on land.

ADAPTATION

ELONGATED LEGS

All waders—from shorebirds such as **avocets** to long-legged waders like **gray herons**—are classed as waterbirds. Most have long legs, with lengthy toes to help them stalk through water, paired with extended bills for probing into the wet mud.

Ardea cinerea

The **Jingwei** is a bird from Chinese mythology that tries to fill the Eastern Sea with twigs and pebbles. It is a symbol of unstoppable determination.

The Water Bird, also known as the **Peyote Bird**, is a symbol of the renewal of life in the tradition of the Plains Indians, including the Arapaho, Apache, Sioux, and Cheyenne.

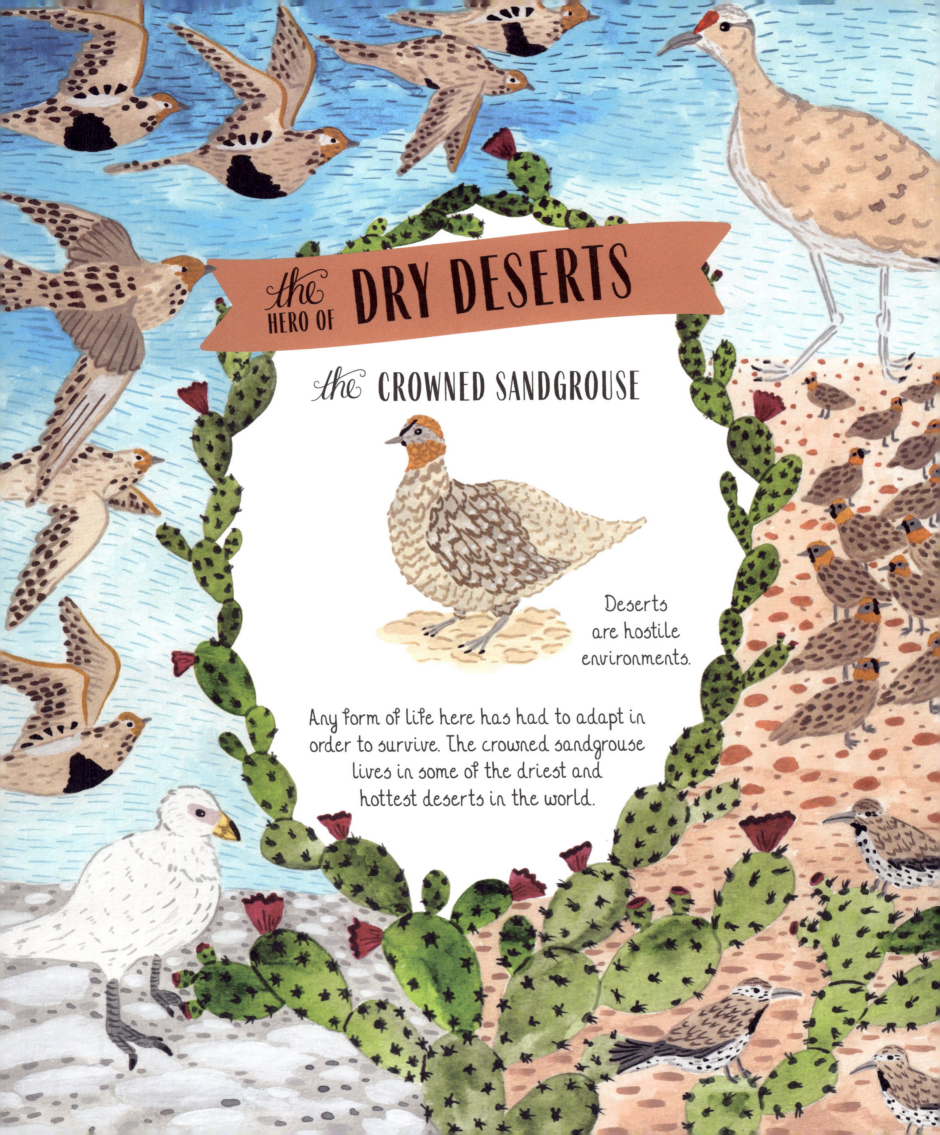

the HERO OF DRY DESERTS

the CROWNED SANDGROUSE

Deserts are hostile environments.

Any form of life here has had to adapt in order to survive. The crowned sandgrouse lives in some of the driest and hottest deserts in the world.

CROWNED SANDGROUSE
Pterocles coronatus

Despite the lack of water, there is life to be found in a desert: Plants like the cactus exist, as well as insects, reptiles, mammals, and, of course, birds. The crowned sandgrouse lives in the harsh deserts of North Africa and South Asia, spending its days quietly searching for seeds under the blazing sun.

HEAT SHIELD
This crowned sandgrouse has tough skin with a dense covering of feathers to **insulate** it from the desert heat. During the hottest parts of the day it will seek shelter under rocks.

Sandgrouse must drink at a **water hole** every day. These risky trips make them vulnerable to predation, so they visit at dawn or dusk.

A **third** of the land on Earth is desert, and these areas are growing.

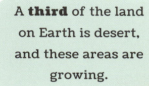

Male sandgrouse **soak up water** in their belly feathers, then return to their chicks, which sip the water droplets.

Deserts are barren landscapes where there is very **little rainfall**: less than 10 inches of rain a year. Not all deserts are hot, though: Did you know that Antarctica is also classified as a desert?

HOW TO SPOT
Like many desert birds, sandgrouse are sandy-colored, which camouflages them well. To find these secretive birds during the day is nearly impossible unless they are flying. The best place to see them is to hide yourself and wait by their favorite water holes. They are nervous birds and will only stop to drink for a few seconds.

ALL ABOUT DESERT BIRDS

Naturally, there is virtually no water to be found in deserts, so birds living there have to find other sources of moisture: Plants, insects, and other prey can all provide vital hydration.

Calypte costae

COSTA'S HUMMINGBIRD
This is one of the few hummingbirds to be found in semiarid deserts and is an important **pollinator** of desert plants.

Alaemon alaudipes

GREATER HOOPOE-LARK
Birds cannot sweat, so instead the greater hoopoe-lark pants through its beak and stands tall to lose heat through its legs.

GREATER ROADRUNNER
Did you know that the famous **Roadrunner** cartoon character is based on a real bird? This member of the cuckoo family is a poor flier but a great sprinter!

Geococcyx californianus

HOUBARA BUSTARD
This desert bird is in danger of **extinction** because hunters have been using large falcons to catch and kill them.

Chlamydotis undulata

DRY DESERTS

DESERT BIRDS AROUND THE WORLD

The large gatherings of sandgrouse at water sources have come to symbolize the gathering together of many tribes in **Bedouin** poetry.

The Alicanto is a mythical nocturnal bird of the deserts of **Atacama** in Chile. Its wings are said to glow at night, and strange lights come from its eyes.

The **Stymphalian bird** is a fierce mythological desert bird thought to originate from Arabia. It has sharpened wingtips that it launches like darts to stab its prey.

The **Thunderbird** is prevalent in the stories of many Indigenous American peoples, including those of the Great Plains. It is a symbol of strength and is said to produce both thunder and lightning.

ADAPTATION

GROUND-DWELLING

To conserve energy, many desert birds prefer to walk or run rather than fly. They are even harder to detect when they stand still like **Temminck's larks** often do.

Eremophila bilopha

DRY DESERTS — 41 — DRY DESERTS

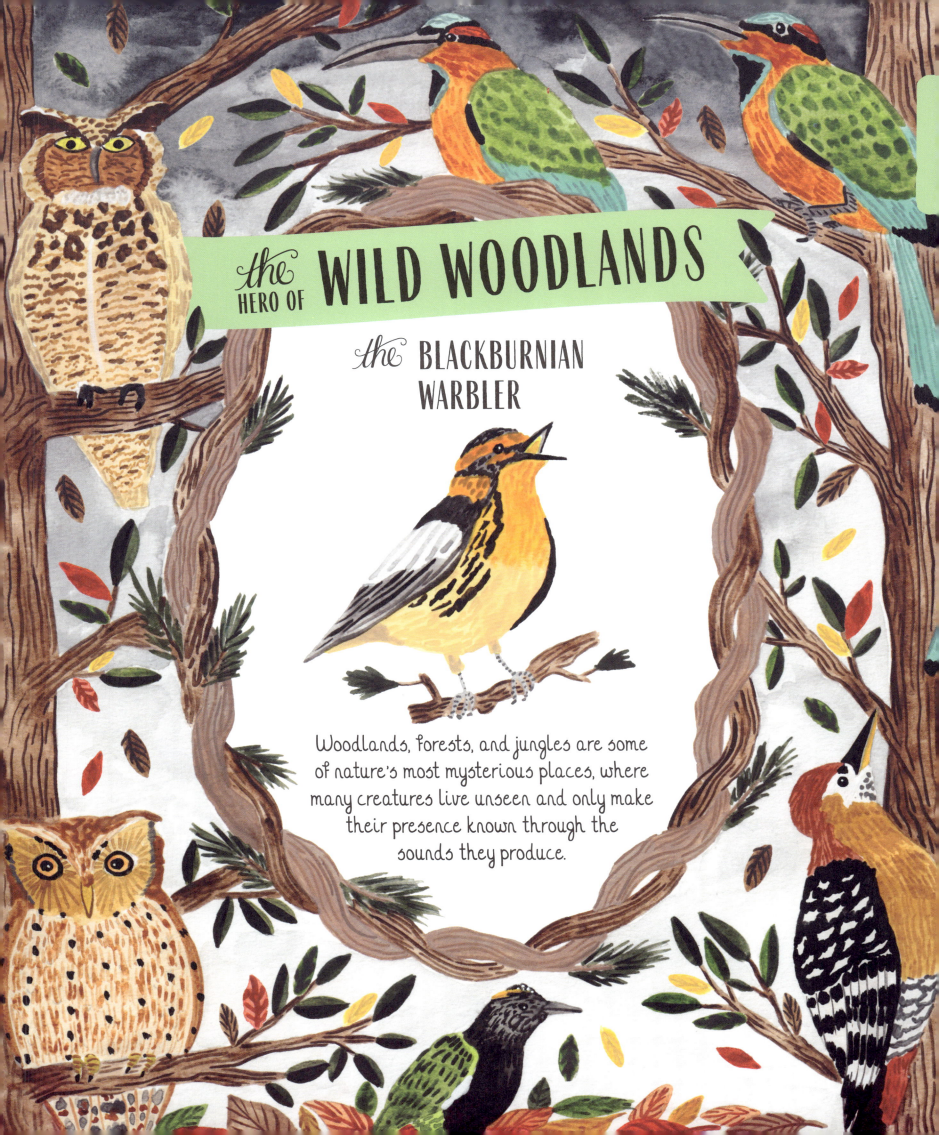

the HERO OF WILD WOODLANDS

the BLACKBURNIAN WARBLER

Woodlands, forests, and jungles are some of nature's most mysterious places, where many creatures live unseen and only make their presence known through the sounds they produce.

BLACKBURNIAN WARBLER
Setophaga fusca

Woodland birds aren't all brown; many are brightly colored. Nevertheless, they can be surprisingly difficult to pick out among the forest foliage—even when they are calling loudly! One of the most glamorous examples is the Blackburnian warbler, from the mixed and coniferous forests of northeastern North America.

COLORFUL CREATURES

Blackburnian warblers migrate from the forests of South America to **breed** in the woods of eastern North America. In the spring, they are eagerly awaited by North American birders as they bring a splash of color to the region.

This little woodland **jewel** is smaller than a sparrow. The males are more brightly colored than the females.

male

Males arrive in the woods first to establish their **territories**.

By the autumn, when they start their migration, the males' plumage has **faded**.

Despite being a fairly common bird, the Blackburnian warbler is under threat from **deforestation** and habitat degradation in both the breeding areas and their wintering grounds.

HOW TO SPOT

You will have a good chance of seeing this beautiful bird from March to May in eastern North America. Many people attend birding festivals in the spring, like the Biggest Week in American Birding held in northwest Ohio, to watch for thousands of small migrating birds heading to their northern forest breeding areas. Finding migrating Blackburnian warblers at these events is always worth celebrating!

ALL ABOUT WOODLAND BIRDS

Woodlands support a wide array of species that have evolved to live among the trees. In tropical forest regions the diversity is even greater, with many more species of animals and plants to be found.

TAWNY OWL

Owls are one of the classic woodland birds, and some species like the tawny owl even live in the woods within our **cities**.

SPOTTED FLYCATCHER

Flycatchers are named for their ability to **catch flies** and other small insects.

ADAPTATION

DRILLING BEAKS

The beaks of **Andean flickers** and other woodpeckers have a chisel-like tip. The birds' spongy skulls absorb the impact of pecking repeatedly on wood. These adaptations help make it a successful family of birds that is found in almost every woodland habitat on the planet except for Australia.

WOODLAND BIRDS AROUND THE WORLD

In ancient Rome, the common magpie was associated with magic and fortune-telling, while in Norse, Irish, and English folklore they are connected to **witchcraft**.

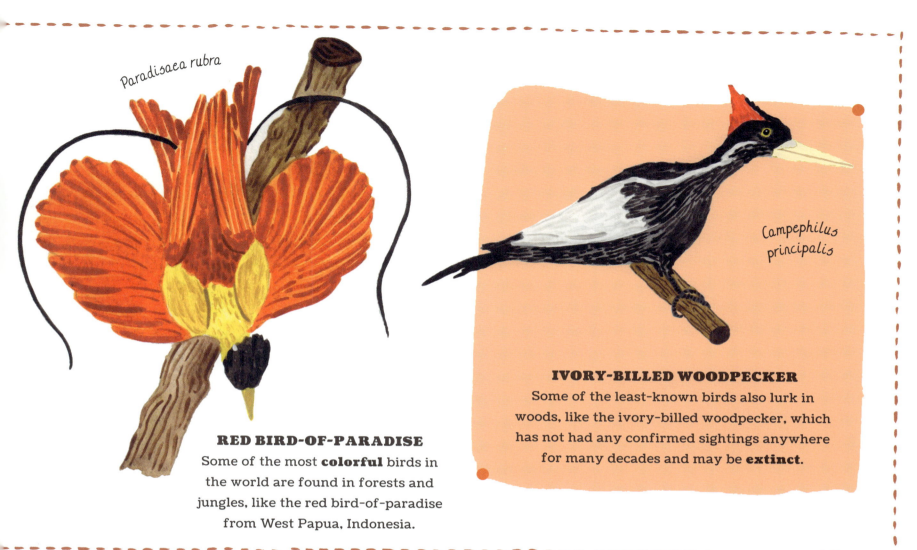

Paradisaea rubra

RED BIRD-OF-PARADISE
Some of the most **colorful** birds in the world are found in forests and jungles, like the red bird-of-paradise from West Papua, Indonesia.

Campephilus principalis

IVORY-BILLED WOODPECKER
Some of the least-known birds also lurk in woods, like the ivory-billed woodpecker, which has not had any confirmed sightings anywhere for many decades and may be **extinct**.

Goldcrests earned the nickname **"woodcock pilots"** partly due to an old English myth about the tiny birds hitching a ride on the backs of migrating Eurasian woodcocks. In fact, the diminutive birds fly hundreds of miles by themselves, making them one of the smallest birds to migrate.

Owls were thought to have **spiritual powers** among many Indigenous American tribes, with connections to death, the afterlife, and rebirth.

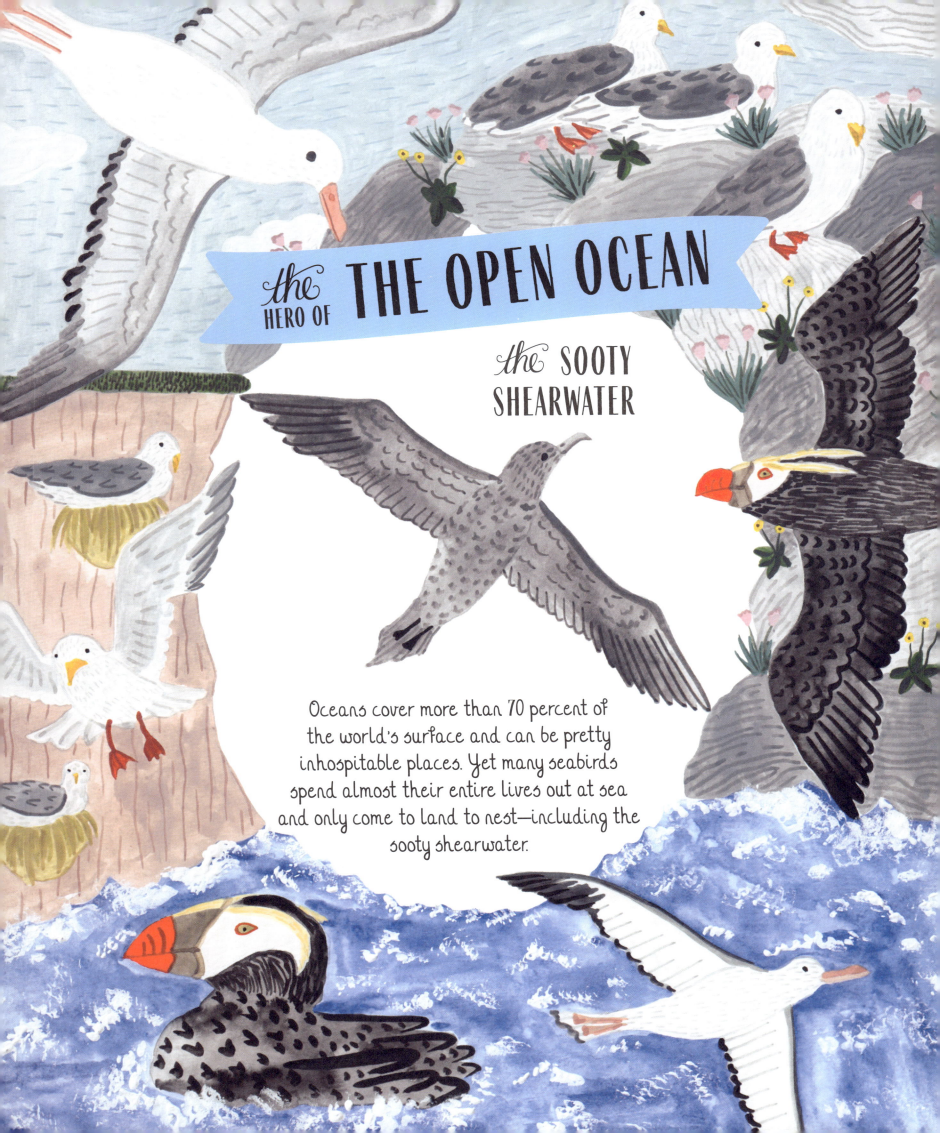

THE OPEN OCEAN

the HERO OF

the SOOTY SHEARWATER

Oceans cover more than 70 percent of the world's surface and can be pretty inhospitable places. Yet many seabirds spend almost their entire lives out at sea and only come to land to nest—including the sooty shearwater.

SOOTY SHEARWATER
Ardenna grisea

Most seabirds are fantastic fliers and skilled at gliding for miles over the ocean waves. Many seabirds are expert divers, too. The sooty shearwater is both of these things, but many of us have never heard of them—let alone seen any in the wild—due to their oceanic way of life.

FLYING UNDERWATER

This medium-size seabird is in the same family as the closely related albatross. These birds have an exceptional sense of smell and curious, **tubelike nostrils** on their bills.

As they don't have access to fresh water, shearwaters drink seawater instead and **"sweat"** the salt through their nostrils.

Shearwaters nest in **burrows** beneath scrub and lay a single egg that is incubated for nearly two months.

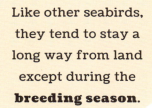

Sooty shearwaters are also strong swimmers and actively **dive** underwater to catch prey. They have been recorded at depths of more than 200 feet.

Like other seabirds, they tend to stay a long way from land except during the **breeding season**.

Famous Hollywood director Alfred Hitchcock based the terrifying flock scenes from his horror film **The Birds** on an actual event in California in 1961, when thousands of sooty shearwaters came ashore during heavy fog.

HOW TO SPOT
Sooty shearwaters can nest in huge colonies. However, though they are noisy birds, their dark plumage makes them difficult to spot at night when they visit their nests. The ideal time to see these birds is when they are migrating across the sea. They are best viewed from a boat out at sea and are occasionally visible from rocky headlands.

ALL ABOUT SEABIRDS

Seabirds have adapted to their tough marine environment in various ways. Some, like shearwaters, are amazing fliers, while others, such as penguins, are completely flightless but are fabulous swimmers.

RED-LEGGED KITTIWAKE
Rissa brevirostris
Although it spends winters at sea, this bird sometimes ventures inland and can be spotted visiting **bird feeders**!

GRAY-HEADED ALBATROSS
This seabird has incredibly long wings and can **drift** for vast distances at sea without ever flapping. It flies this way in order to save energy.

Thalassarche chrysostoma

CAPE GANNET
A gannet can close its **nostrils** when diving to prevent water getting in.

Morus capensis

Pelecanoides magellani

MAGELLANIC DIVING PETREL
The curious Magellanic diving petrel, with its sturdy little body and **whirring flight**, is actually related to albatrosses.

Alle alle

LITTLE AUKS
This bird may be called "little" but it eats **60,000 copepods** every day!

SEABIRDS AROUND THE WORLD

The white tern is sometimes called the **navigator's** best friend because it has been said to lead tired sailors home.

Hawaiian mythology includes stories of frigate birds and tropic birds being **messengers** for the gods.

The mysterious **Saint Kenneth** from the 6th century is said to have been raised by black-headed gulls after being found as a baby floating off the coast of Wales.

Albatrosses are thought of as being the souls of **lost sailors**, so killing them would be regarded as bad luck.

ADAPTATION

OILY FEATHERS

All seabirds have waterproof plumages that they maintain by spreading their feathers with a special oil from a gland near the base of their tails. Many also have mainly white bellies and underwings that make them invisible to their fish prey when viewed against the sky. The diminutive **ancient murrelet** is a classic example.

Synthliboramphus antiquus

the HERO OF GRASSLANDS

the CHESTNUT-COLLARED LONGSPUR

Grassland habitats are especially loved by seed-eating birds. And where there is grass there are insects, too. The chestnut-collared longspur—a classic bird of the North American Great Plains—loves feasting on both!

CHESTNUT-COLLARED LONGSPUR
CALCARIUS ORNATUS

Grasslands are disappearing at an alarming rate. The vast prairies that existed in the American Midwest and are home to longspurs have largely been transformed into agricultural land. But when left to prosper, grasslands—even very small ones in your yard—can support an amazing ecosystem that can sometimes be seen if you stop and wait patiently.

HIDDEN FLOCKS
In their grassland home, chestnut-collared longspurs forage on the ground, gathering in **flocks** during the winter. They can be very difficult to detect as they like hiding in very dense grass, where they are camouflaged thanks to their brown plumage.

Males fly into the air and perform a fluttering **flight song** to protect their territory during breeding season.

female

The males have **darker** plumage than the females.

"**Longspur**" refers to the bird's long, thin claw on the hind toe of each foot.

Like many **seedeaters**, this longspur feeds its young with insects to give them the protein they need to help them survive their first year of life.

HOW TO SPOT
The chestnut-collared longspur is a mysterious bird. Many birders have never seen one, partly because the population has declined by more than 87 percent since the 1960s. But these shy birds will fly up in a group at the last minute when you unknowingly walk near them, and they can then hide themselves from view again, even in very short grass!

GRASSLANDS

ALL ABOUT GRASSLAND BIRDS

Between 20 and 40 percent of the world's landmass is covered in grasslands, but these areas are very vulnerable to destruction from human development, overgrazing, fires, and climate change.

GREATER PRAIRIE CHICKEN

These birds thrive best in **undisturbed grasslands** in North America. They are now endangered due to their habitat being developed for agriculture.

Tympanuchus cupido

Buteo regalis

Anthus pratensis

FERRUGINOUS HAWK

There are several **birds of prey** that specialize in grassland habitats, including this hawk, which hunts small rodents, snakes, and birds.

MEADOW PIPIT

This common grassland bird from Europe can even be encountered in small patches of long grass in **urban areas** during the winter.

GRASSLAND BIRDS AROUND THE WORLD

Eagle festivals are held across the grasslands of Central Asia, which are known as the **steppes**. Eagle hunters (burkitshi) come together to compete with specially trained golden eagles.

GRASSLANDS

DICKCISSEL

When allowed to grow and flourish, grassland habitats are especially loved by seed-eating birds like the dickcissel, which relish filling themselves up with the **seeds** of the vegetation growing there.

Spiza americana

ADAPTATION

IMITATION

Some grassland birds sound like insects when they sing, such as the **grasshopper sparrow**, which makes a quiet, insect-like buzzing sound. The sparrow's predator, the **Northern harrier**, has developed keen senses of sight and hearing to help it locate its prey.

Ammodramus savannarum *Circus hudsonius*

Crex crex

CORNCRAKE

Many of the birds living in grasslands, like the corncrake, are **ground-dwellers** that spend their time looking for food and nesting on the ground as secretly as possible.

In an Argentine children's story, a magic tree grows in the middle of the grasslands there, known as the **pampas**. An evil bird sleeps atop the tree to stop the rain from falling.

Grouse are used to identify clans in some North American cultures, such as the Prairie Chicken clans of the Mandan and Hidatsa. The feathers are traditionally arranged into a **bustle** to be worn when dancing.

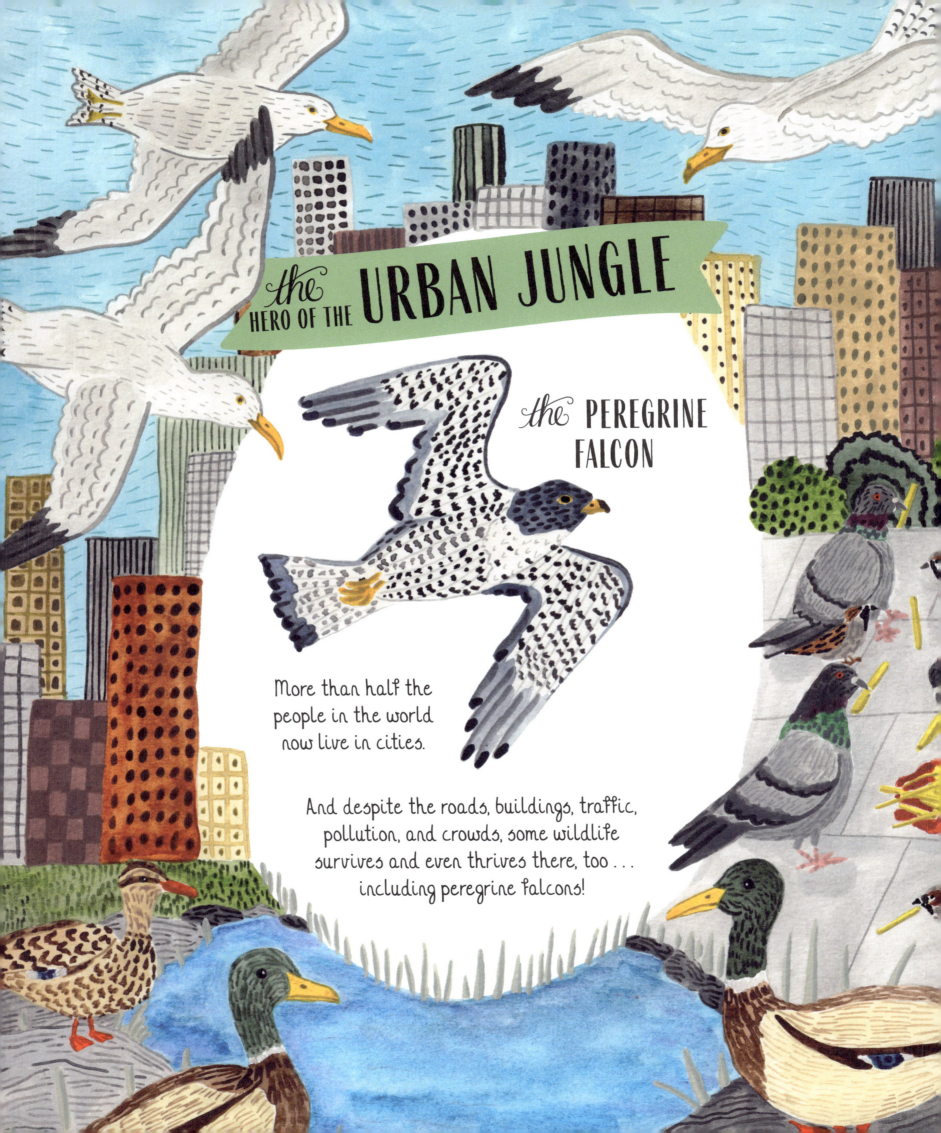

the HERO OF THE URBAN JUNGLE

the PEREGRINE FALCON

More than half the people in the world now live in cities.

And despite the roads, buildings, traffic, pollution, and crowds, some wildlife survives and even thrives there, too... including peregrine falcons!

PEREGRINE FALCON
Falco peregrinus

People tend to think of feral pigeons as the only birds in cities, but ornithologists believe that up to 20 percent of the world's 11,000 bird species live among us in urban areas—including the peregrine falcon. So, next time you go outside, look up: You might be surprised at what you see!

URBAN CREATURE
Many peregrine falcons have now swapped their lives in the wilderness, nesting on wild, inaccessible cliff ledges, for **urban** existences, nesting on the roofs and ledges that our tall buildings provide.

This species was in serious danger of extinction across much of North America and Europe because of agricultural chemicals. Thankfully, these were banned and the bird population began to **recover**.

"Peregrine" means **wandering**—indeed, a peregrination is a journey. This species can migrate over 15,000 miles every year.

The peregrine falcon also happens to be the **fastest** animal on the planet! When diving after prey, it can reach speeds of 200 miles per hour or more: That's as fast as the bullet trains in Japan!

HOW TO SPOT
If you live in a small town, check your local church spire or any funnel stacks on industrial estates. New York City and London have the largest urban populations of peregrine falcons in the world, with at least 25 pairs in each city. The best place to find them is in the very heart of each metropolis, as they can sometimes be seen sitting discreetly for long periods on the ledges of skyscrapers.

ALL ABOUT URBAN BIRDS

Far from being devoid of birdlife, some urban areas have recorded a phenomenal number of species. One of the best cities in the world for urban birding is Nairobi, Kenya, where more than 600 species have been seen.

FERAL PIGEON

Probably the most **abundant** bird in cities around the world is the feral pigeon. They breed so quickly that they can be thought of as pests.

Columba livia forma urbana

HOUSE SPARROW

As its name suggests, the house sparrow has adapted to live **alongside humans** and is found in cities across the world.

Passer domesticus

MALLARD

Your local pond or lake is sure to attract birdlife, and the versatile, **adaptable** mallard is found all over the northern hemisphere.

Anas platyrhynchos

HERRING GULL

Gulls are increasingly choosing to live in urban environments over their traditional coastal habitats, finding more **reliable** options for nesting sites and food in such places.

Larus argentatus

RING-NECKED PARAKEET

Large flocks of parakeets live in urban locations around southern England because some that were kept as pets **escaped** into the wild!

Psittacula krameri

THE URBAN JUNGLE

ADAPTATION

Parus major

LOUD CALLS

As an adaptation to city living, many species have learned to sing louder to attract the attention of potential mates. Research has even shown that some species, like **urban great tits**, not only sing louder but also differently. In fact, great tits living in quieter rural areas have begun to respond less to the city singers and vice versa.

URBAN BIRDS AROUND THE WORLD

In India, **black kites** came to thrive in cities like Delhi thanks to a religious practice carried out there that involved making an offering of meat to birds.

In 2020, a tiny saw-whet owl was found in New York's famous **Rockefeller Center** Christmas tree. "Rocky" appeared to have been living in the tree when it was cut down, and was later released back into the wild.

Six **ravens** have been kept as residents at the Tower of London since the reign of Charles II in the 17th century. Legend has it that if the Tower's ravens are lost or fly away, the Crown, the kingdom, and the Tower itself will fall.

THE URBAN JUNGLE

KAKAPO
Strigops habroptila

Today, despite conservation projects, there are still fewer than 300 kakapos in the wild. The species is in critical danger of extinction due to habitat loss and overhunting by creatures like dogs, cats, rats, and stoats, which early settlers brought with them to New Zealand.

The kakapo is one of the planet's longest-living birds, with a life span of up to **90 years**!

The name kakapo (often written as kākāpō) is a **Māori** word. Kākā means "parrot" and pō means "night."

A MOST UNUSUAL PARROT

Also known as the owl parrot, the kakapo is large, nocturnal, and only found in New Zealand, where it is very rare. Not only is it the world's only flightless parrot, it is also the **heaviest** parrot on Earth, weighing as much as 9 pounds.

HOW TO SPOT
This parrot is one of the hardest to find in the wild.

You may not actually see the bird but might come across signs of its existence, such as hearing its calls, finding a discarded feather, or coming across some droppings. The most successful conservation scheme designed to save the species from extinction has been the Kākāpō Recovery Plan, which was started in 1996. Its first job was to relocate the existing birds to predator-free islands. These birds were tagged and are monitored around the clock.

During its evolution, the kakapo became **flightless** because it lived on an island with few natural predators, so there was no need to fly away!

This is a ground-dwelling bird. It searches for food by **walking** and climbing trees.

CONSERVATION — 59 — CONSERVATION

ALL ABOUT CONSERVATION

Habroptila wallacii

There are many individuals and conservation organizations across the globe working hard to protect birds. Combined, these groups watch over 8.5 million square miles of protected areas in the world—at least 17 percent of Earth's land environments.

There are numerous success stories due to conservation—but so many more birds that need our help to survive.

INVISIBLE RAIL
Almost 15 species of rail have become extinct since 1600, and the invisible rail's numbers are also dwindling because the bird's **range is restricted** to a small island in Indonesia where its habitat is under threat.

COMMON REDSTART
Weather altered by **climate change**, together with intensive farming practices that reduce nesting sites, are causing common redstart numbers to plummet.

Phoenicurus phoenicurus

CONSERVATION AROUND THE WORLD

The **yellow-breasted bunting** used to be abundant in China but was hunted almost to extinction. It is now protected, and its numbers have slowly begun to increase again.

Emberiza aureola

Himantopus novaezelandiae

The **black stilt**, found in New Zealand, would almost certainly have gone extinct if it weren't for a conservation program that bred the birds in captivity and reintroduced them into the wild.

Ara glaucogularis

The **blue-throated macaw** was thought to be extinct until it was rediscovered in a nature reserve in Bolivia in 1992. Now, there are between 50 and 250 of these beautiful birds left in the world in this single spot.

TURQUOISE COTINGA

Deforestation means that the turquoise cotinga's already small habitat in Central America is being broken up and destroyed, causing its numbers to decrease.

Cotinga ridgwayi

Streptopelia turtur

EUROPEAN TURTLE DOVE

Overhunting in the Mediterranean and North Africa combined with habitat destruction of its European breeding grounds—especially in the UK—means the European turtle dove is now threatened with extinction.

ADAPTATION

Birds are very sensitive to human actions. In many cases, their habitats are changing faster than they are able to adapt, and currently 49 percent of all bird species are in decline, with several in grave danger of extinction.

Habitat loss, climate change, the trapping of wild birds to be sold as pets, and overhunting are all making the problems worse.

To help reverse this downward trend, it's we humans who need to adapt our behavior. We have to **conserve more habitats**, halt illegal logging, ask hunters to be more responsible, and launch conservation projects in our urban areas to connect more people to the fight that nature faces.

After being abundant in Great Britain during the Middle Ages, the population of the elegant **red kite** was reduced to a handful of pairs in Wales by the 1970s. Young birds were reintroduced from Spain in the 1980s, and now there are several thousand pairs across Britain.

Milvus milvus

The **California condor** is critically endangered. A careful breeding campaign carried out in American zoos has produced chicks that have been reintroduced into the wild and now help its recovery.

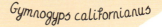
Gymnogyps californianus

CONSERVATION · 61 · CONSERVATION

GLOSSARY

AIR THERMAL – a column of air rising through the sky

BARBS – hooked branches within a feather that keep it stiff and smooth

BREED – to mate and produce chicks

CAMOUFLAGE – coloration that helps something blend in with its environment

CANOPY – the upper layer of trees

COLONY – a group of one species of bird

COMMUNAL – shared by many

COURTSHIP DISPLAY – behavior that aims to attract a mate

CRÈCHE – a place where many young are cared for together

CREST – feathers that stand out around a bird's head

DEFORESTATION – the removal of trees from an area of land

DIMINUTIVE – small

ECOSYSTEM – a community of plants and animals that interact

EXTINCT – no longer in existence

EYESPOT – a marking that looks like an eye

GLIDE – to fly without flapping

GROUND-DWELLING – spending most of its time on the floor

INSULATE – to stop heat from entering or escaping

MIGRATE – move from one place to another in a seasonal pattern

ORNITHOLOGIST – a scientist who studies birds

PECTORAL MUSCLES – muscles across a bird's chest that connect to its wings

PENNANT FEATHER – a long, tapering feather

PLUMAGE – a bird's covering of feathers

PREEN – to clean and groom feathers with the beak

PROBE – to examine by penetrating

RAPTOR – a bird of prey

RUFF – feathers around the neck

SHAFT – the long, stiff, central part of a feather

TALON – a long, sharp claw

TERRITORY – the area controlled by an individual or group

TUFT – a group of feathers growing closely together

WEBBED – describes toes that are connected by skin

WINGSPAN – the length of a bird's wings from one tip to the other

FURTHER READING

Links to online resources to learn more:

Birdlife Australia – www.birdlife.org.au
BirdLife International – birdlife.org
Darwin Foundation – darwinfoundation.org
Defenders of Wildlife – defenders.org
International Union for Conservation of Nature – iucn.org
National Audubon Society – audubon.org
National Geographic – nationalgeographic.com
Royal Society for the Protection of Birds – rspb.org.uk
World Wildlife Fund – worldwildlife.org

To Mum, thank you for supporting my insatiable desire to learn about birds throughout my life —D.L.

To my wonderful Dad, the OG birder —S.B.M.

The illustrations in this book were created in watercolor and gouache paints.
Set in A Thousand Years, Coustard, Farmhand, Haute, and Moonflower.

Library of Congress Control Number 2023950216
ISBN 978-1-4197-7346-4

Text © 2024 David Lindo
Illustrations © 2024 Sara Boccaccini Meadows
Book design by Nicola Price
Cover © 2024 Magic Cat

First published in the United Kingdom in 2024 by Magic Cat Publishing Ltd. First published in North America in 2024 by Magic Cat Publishing, an imprint of ABRAMS. All rights reserved. No portion of this book may be reproduced, stored in a retrieval system, or transmitted in any form or by any means, mechanical, electronic, photocopying, recording, or otherwise, without written permission from the publisher.

Printed and bound in China
10 9 8 7 6 5 4 3 2 1

Abrams books are available at special discounts when purchased in quantity for premiums and promotions as well as fundraising or educational use. Special editions can also be created to specification. For details, contact specialsales@abramsbooks.com or the address below.

ABRAMS The Art of Books
195 Broadway, New York, NY 10007
abramsbooks.com